Griner

By Earl Ofari Hutchinson

Copyright 2022

Table of Contents

Introduction

NBA superstar Lebron James took much heat for his off-the-cup quip about detained WNBA superstar Brittney Griner. In a bit of random chatter on the TV series, "The Shop," on July 14 James wondered aloud if America had her back for not immediately bringing her home. When the predictable firestorm of criticism hit, James quickly backpedaled. In a *tweet*, he praised "our beautiful country" and made clear he was not knocking the government for its action or inaction on Griner was intended.

James wasn't too far off with his initial quip. Not because of what prompted him to muse aloud about the country. It had nothing to do with America's supposed inaction on Griner. In fact, President Biden to his credit repeatedly publicly spoke out about Griner. He protested her detention, pledged to do whatever he could to secure her release, and called her detention "wrongful." Biden sent a letter on July 6, 2022 to Griner's wife, Cherelle Griner, and offered profuse assurance as he put it that he was " working to secure Brittney's release as soon as possible."

There was also much talk about a prisoner swap to get her back home.

Griner for her part was anything but stoic about her plight. She fired off a handwritten letter to Biden thanking him for his support. But she made it clear that she was terrified about being locked up in a Russian jail with no on-the-ground support there from her family and friends.

*****

Griner had languished in a Russian jail since February 17, 2022. She was arrested at the Moscow airport, jailed, and charged with illicit drug possession. The drug was a cannabis-derived vape cartridges. Though it is not a prohibited drug in the

U.S., and by the World Anti-Doping Agency, it mattered little to the Russians. She appeared in court several times in the months that followed. Russian authorities claimed to see the high profile, African American lesbian WNBA superstar playing in Russia for a Russian team as nothing more than a lawbreaker.

It was much more than that. Her case was the perfect issues storm. The issues were race, gender, same-sex identity, celebrity, drugs, political jockeying and brinkmanship, and a raging war. There was far more to Griner than drugs.

In *Griner*, noted political analyst Earl Ofari Hutchinson goes beneath the surface in her case. He examines the issues of race, gender, celebrity, the disparities in men's and women's pro sports, politics, and war that are deeply embedded in the Griner saga. Hutchinson places her arrest against the backdrop of the escalation in tensions between Russia and the U.S. over Russia's invasion of Ukraine. Hutchinson asks did that make her a political pawn in the jockeying between the two countries over the war as many charged?

Griner is a fast, paced, laser look at how one pro basketball player, became for the moment, much more than just a basketball player.

1

Why Griner Was There

One question repeatedly was asked by many causal observers from the moment Griner was arrested and charged with illegal drug possession in Russia. The question: "Why was she in Russia?" There were two reasons. One it was the offseason for the women of the WNBA.

This reason took an extremely poor second to the other reason Griner and many other female American basketball players were in Russia and other foreign countries. Money! Griner for instance had played not one but seven seasons in Russia. She bagged about one million dollars each season for playing there. That was far, far more than she could make in the WNBA. To be exact, it was quadruple the estimated two hundred thousand plus that she made annually in the WNBA.

The howl over the gaping pay disparity between what female pro basketball players make in comparison to NBA players has been long and loud. Griner was a bona fide superstar, a seven-time all-pro. Yet her salary was about one-twentieth of what an average NBA player NBA makes.

Here's some perspective on the cavernous difference between men's and women's pro ball players. The NBA Utah Jazz's Rudy Gobert and Griner have played about the same length of time in their leagues. They are both top talent centers and were multiple all-star picks. That's where the similarity ends. **Spotrac** put Gobert's base salary for the 2021-22 NBA season at $35,344,828. That's $431,034 a season game.

Griner made slightly more than half of that not for one game but for the entire season! Keep in mind, that she was one of the highest-paid WNBA players.

*****

That's just the tip of the iceberg. Griner by the standard of the WNBA is super rich. She's paid double what the average WNBA player makes. The counter to those who scream about the glaring disparity in pay and attention between men's and women's pro sports is that the WNBA, women's sport, can hardly be compared to the NBA, men's sport.

The men's pro and college sports are the cash cows of sport. Millions pay to attend and view on TV their games. There are just far more commercial bucks to be made and paid in men's sport than in women's sport. That first and foremost includes the NBA versus the WNBA.

The other counter to the critics is that if the fans are in far greater attendance at men's contests than women's that means the revenue from ticket sales, media coverage, and advertising, is far greater. One news article on the issue was blunt. It noted that for every dollar that the media, fans, and corporate sponsors plow into men's sport, about a penny goes to women's professional sports.

The NBA generates about $7.4 billion in revenue, while the WNBA generated about $60 million in 2021. The **average ticket price for an NBA game** was $89 **in comparison to the WNBA's $17.42 in 2021**.

*****

In April 2019, the WNBA believed that it had made a huge stride toward attaining some semblance of equity in men's versus women's pro basketball pay and visibility. The *CBS Sports Network* agreed to televise an array of WNBA games. That was in addition to the deal the league had with *ESPN* to provide TV coverage. The deal meant greater exposure. The hope was that would translate into greater fan attendance. Part of that hope for a greater exposure boost was realized. Ratings soared from the previous year, 2018. The other part, the hoped-for bump up in fan attendance didn't happen. The fans continued to stay away in droves. The average attendance for a game was far under 10,000 for the league. A 2021 USC/Purdue University study found that almost all TV-covered sports news or highlights were of men's sports stories.

There was one more pernicious spin-off from the top-heavy coverage of men's sports and the ignoring of women's sports. This perpetuated the ancient gender stereotype that women's play even at the professional level was different and that the women were less physically talented and athletic than the men. So, why then so the counter argument goes expect fans to pack arenas to see a poor imitation of men's pro sport that supposedly women offered on the court.

One analyst came closest to a much-denied truth about the attitudes among many men and more than a few women held about men and women players. He summarized why the distancing, if not aversion from many to women's pro basketball,

"The fact is a lot of men don't want to watch the WNBA because they think it's boring. How do I know? I've asked. They are used to high-flying dunks and blocks and fast-paced wheeling and dealing on the court. That's what they want in a basketball game. But the only female baller that can really throw down is Brittney Griner. And guys think she's too manly. But they want dunks. Yet they don't want girls to be overly athletic."

*****

The instant the last whistle blows on the last game of the WNBA season, the women players head for the airports to board flights to other countries such as China, Turkey, Greece, Spain, France, Israel, and of course Russia to fatten their bank accounts. The increased pay that they receive in foreign countries such as Russia though higher than the WNBA still pales in comparison to the pay of the men in the NBA not to mention what the men receive when they venture overseas to play in professional leagues in foreign countries.

Yet, the women gladly sign up to play for the foreign teams. It gives them a sense that they are being paid more in commensurate with what they feel they are worth, and their talents should command than in the U.S.

For the time being the WNBA's drive in 2021 to uplift women's basketball's popularity wouldn't change the immediate fact that half of all WNBA players feel compelled to go overseas during the off-season to play for higher pay in foreign locales. Australian professional basketball player for the Los Angeles Sparks, Liz Cambage, told why. She said that she makes 5 to 8 times more overseas than she does in the WNBA. "It's hard when you have the best league in the world, but we're not treated like the best athletes in the world."

The WNBA, some corporate sponsors, and fans have taken the complaints of the pay disparity seriously. In 2020, agreements between the league and the players got a major pay hike. That put the average pay a player received for the first time over six figures per player with additional bonuses and incentives. Two years later, in February 2022, the league raised tens of millions more for what it called "brand elevation and marketing" translated: make the league more marketable.

The WNBA's efforts to slightly narrow the gross financial inequality between men's and women's professional basketball are commendable. However, it is a long-term project that will remain problematic in markedly closing the gap given the towering inherent gender bias within professional sports.

There was no mystery why Griner no matter how great her talent had to pack up and head for Russia year after year. The dollars were there, and not in the U.S.

2

Russia, Griner and, Homophobia

In February 2022, the Russian Justice Ministry was direct. It blasted the Russian LGBTQ Network for allegedly spreading LGBT views. In a lawsuit, it demanded that the country's biggest LGBTQ rights groups be shut down. The Ministry didn't stop there. It used an ominous term considering the 70-decade murderous rule of Russian dictator Joseph Stalin and the Communist Party, that it wanted to "liquidate "the legal foundation that ran the group. The suit was tossed out-for the moment. But there was little doubt that the Russian government would not stop until it put the group out of business—or worse.

Even though the authorities were thwarted for the moment in their move against the group, it didn't alter the fact that Russian officials saw LGBTQ views as "alien" to Russian values, meaning, of course, traditional family roles. The Ministry continued its war of words by branding the group and its advocacy as "foreign agents." The government attack underscored the grim reality of life for gays in Russia,

"If you're gay, as long as you hide it, as long as you do not speak up … it's OK, but if you speak up … it becomes a very serious problem," an LGBTQ leader said. "The Russian government is ready to tolerate gay people as long as they're in the closet."

In the closet or not, that didn't mean much to at least forty persons who Russian authorities arrested in 2019. Two of them reportedly were tortured and killed. Their crime. They were LGBT in Chechnya. The terror was so great that LGBT activists in the country moved quickly to spirit hundreds of other LGBT persons out of the region.

The horrific action by Russian officials in their persecution of gays was hardly new. Two years earlier, police in Chechnya with Russian official approval rounded up hordes of men they claimed were gay, subjecting them to the usual torture, and jailing's. They even encouraged their families to murder them, through what they dubbed "honor killings." Many terrified Russians fled the country and sought asylum in other Western European nations. Putin was challenged on the reign of terror against gays. He promised an investigation, and then promptly whitewashed it.

But then why would anyone expect any action from him? He virtually made LGBT bias a state policy in 2013 when he signed what came to be known as a "gay propaganda" measure into federal law. The law prohibited the distribution of alleged "propaganda of non-traditional sexual relations" to minors. Russia's discriminatory law weaponized the language of care and protection against an already-marginalized group. That fueled even greater stigma, harassment, and violence against LGBT people in Russia.

*****

The nagging question in the Griner case with that backdrop was could the open hostility toward

LGBT persons from Putin on down factor in her safety? Worse, could it pose a threat to her timely release? Those questions were difficult to answer. Putin and Russian authorities certainly never mentioned Griner's sexual orientation when they mentioned her at all.

That would have left them wide open to the charge that she was being singled out for harsh punishment not because she allegedly broke Russia's drug laws, but because of her sexual orientation. It would also call greater global attention to Russia's horrid view of and treatment of gays.

Oscar winning filmmaker, Ben Proudfoot, was one genuinely concerned that Griner's sexual orientation would put her at risk in Russia. His documentary *Queen of Basketball* on women's professional basketball won an Academy Award in 2022. He was one of the first to implore President Biden to do all he could to secure her release.

There was a special urgency in his plea.
Griner was not just openly, unapologetically gay,
with an outspoken wife. She was one of the most
visible, and high-profile advocates of gay rights
within the world of women's professional sports. In
July 2017, she led a fundraising drive for the
Phoenix LGBTQ youth center where she had done
volunteer work. The center had been torched under
suspicious circumstances. The center served lesbian,
gay, bisexual, and transgender youth ages 14 to 24.

"I remember thinking that's sad that someone would
do that," Griner said, "This is a safe zone and safe
spot for LGBT community and youth. It's a place
that helps so many. Not having a safe zone or people
to talk to or be around others in the same position is
toughest thing ever."

Griner was showered with honors and
recognition by LGBT organizations and activists for
her championing of LGBT rights and causes. This
was topped by her being chosen to be the **been the**

grand marshal of the Phoenix Pride parade in 2014. Her high-profile gay rights activism was even more remarkable in that she worked tirelessly in a state, Arizona, with a governor who likely wouldn't feel the least bit uncomfortable with Putin's hard-line views on gays.

A day before the observance of International Transgender Day of Visibility, Arizona Republican Governor Doug Ducey in March 2022 signed two bills that targeted transgender youths. One of the laws scaled back minors' access to gender-affirming health care; the other banned transgender women and girls from competing on women's and girls' teams at all public schools and some private schools.

The Arizona governor wasn't alone. GOP governors in Oklahoma, Iowa and South Dakota have signed into law bills establishing similar sports bans. In 2021, Alabama, Arkansas, Florida, Mississippi, Montana, Tennessee, Texas, and West Virginia enacted comparable bans.

Even closer to home, there was Griner's father. When she came out publicly that she was gay, he hit the roof. He shouted that he "wasn't raising any lesbian." Griner was crushed. She later told a friend, *"My dad always told me to just be who I was, but I don't think he knew exactly how I took it. He finally got on board that either you accept your daughter and take her for what she is, and you unconditionally love her, or you're not going to have her."*

Whether it was Russia or Arizona where she played, or her own father's initial revulsion, the pattern was the same. With or without her celebrity pro sports status, her many supporters were right to be concerned about how she would fare when they stood in a court docket in a country that held such open scorn for LGBT individuals.

*****

There was more cause for concern about her fate. Griner was not just a Black, gay sports star. She played in a sport, pro basketball, and a league, the WNBA, that often drew open and subtle snickers and wisecracks from many about being a game that is dominated by tall, Black, and a few openly lesbian athletes. The irony of that was that during the first decade of the league's inception it did everything it could to carefully market the league as a wholesome, family values league whose players had boyfriends, husbands, and significant others.

This problem with the WNBA's tortured wholesome image remaking campaign was not lost on U.S. Soccer team captain Megan Rapinoe. She was applauded when she spoke out on women's and LGBTQ+ issues within professional sports. But it was a far different story when it came to Blacks such as Griner.

"When it comes to U.S. women's soccer, the general perception is that — let's face it — we're the white girls next door, "said Rapinoe," The straight, 'cute,' 'unthreatening,' 'suburban' white girls next door."

In many circles in the U.S. and certainly in Russia, Griner hardly fit that bill. She and her identity were just too threatening to many. Putin and Russian officials were right at the top of the list of those offended.

3
From Russia Without Love

Russian President Vladimir Putin speaking through a spokesperson in June 2022, hotly denied that Griner was a "hostage," "a political prisoner," or a "political pawn." These were among the choice charges leveled at the Russians in jailing Griner. The Putin spokesperson went further. He claimed that she was treated no differently or viewed any differently than any other Russian arrested and jailed who was accused of drug possession and dealing. "Why should we make an exemption for a foreign citizen?" he added.

Biden, Vice President Kamala Harris, and a legion of other U.S. political officials begged to differ with Russian officials. They spoke out, demanded her release, and turned the case over to the State

Department Presidential Envoy for Hostage Affairs for handling.

Griner was branded by many as a political pawn or hostage for very compelling reasons. The timing of her arrest was one. She was arrested less than a week before Putin and the Russians launched their brutal invasion of Ukraine. Biden and U.S. officials immediately went on the attack. They lambasted Putin for the invasion and later clamped tough economic sanctions on Russia. Putin called the action akin to an act of war.

Griner had enough name recognition as a long-time top women's pro sports star that her arrest was bound to draw international attention. This could possibly serve as an embarrassment for the U.S., and a potential diversion from criticism of Russia's war.

A second reason for suspicion that politics was involved was her jailing. There were other options. Griner could have been refused entry to the country and sent home. Or, after her arrest she

could have had a speedy court date and a
determination made

28

whether she would or should stand trial. Instead, the case took on all the signs of a case that would be deliberately drug out.

U.S. Embassy officials were not even allowed to see her until five weeks after her detainment. That delay so outraged U.S.'s Russian Ambassador, John Sullivan, that he took to *Twitter* on May 17, 2022, "For the third time in a month, Russian authorities have denied an embassy visit to the detained U.S. citizen Brittney Griner. This is unacceptable. We call on the government to provide timely consular access in line with Russia's international and bilateral obligations."

*****

The reasons for the foot-dragging in the case for some seemed to go beyond the normal time frame of the law for disposing of a case that on the surface seemed to be a relatively minor offense. If it was an offense at all since the drug is legal in the U.S. and the international athletic associations that set the rules on what athletes can and can't use legally do not prohibit the cannabis oil CBD's use. Griner insisted that she had a doctor's prescription for use of the oil.

Experts on Russian law and its court system were leery and suspicious. They contended that there was no rule of law in Russia as in the West. Decisions in legal cases of concern to the government are made from on high. Meaning by top political officials.

This intense speculation did not mean that Griner was a political victim. Or anything other than she was another horrible example of someone caught in Russia's corrupt, overburdened legal system. Other than the one brief statement by a Putin spokesperson on her case, there was almost no mention of her in the Russian press.

Griner pleaded guilty to the charges. That seemed to be a step toward depoliticizing whatever political drama there was in her case. However, the blunt fact was that six months after her arrest and plea bargain, she still languished in a Russian cell in mid-July 2022. The suspicion of political intrigue in her case grew more intense

31

after a court appearance in which there were glowing statements of support for her from the Russian team owners and officials whom she played for for several seasons.

They virtually begged on hands and knees for her release, calling her an exemplary teammate, role model, and a player who did much to elevate women's professional basketball in Russia. That didn't move officials.

In mid-July 2022, Russian officials were still scheduling more hearings for her, presumably to allow time for her defense to present its case. In between politics again intruded when the Russian Foreign Ministry issued a statement that it "was ready to work with the U.S. on a possible exchange and urged Washington to abandon attempts to exert pressure on Russia and not speculate on this 'sensitive matter.'" The statement tossed the political ball at the U.S. and flatly said that the U.S., not Russia was seeking to make Griner's case a political issue.

✱✱✱✱✱

Meanwhile, WNBA officials took the hint from the swirl of controversy surrounding her case. They issued the obligatory statements in her support. However, league officials were mum on any specific plans they had if there were any to facilitate her release.

Whether she was a political pawn or just a garden variety offender that ran afoul of Russian law, the whiff of politics would continue to hang in the air. If for no other reason than her case was set against the backdrop of the bitter round of accusations and recrimination between the U.S. and Russa over Ukraine as well as other geopolitical hotspots the two countries clashed and jockeyed over.

As long as Griner remained in a Russian cell, and tensions, continued to rise, the real or imagined use of her case for political reasons would always remain within the realm of possibility. With the U.S.

strongly committed to providing weapons and support to Ukraine and the strengthening of the NATO alliance against Russia, Griner would assure that possibility.

Conclusion

On July 15, 2022, Poor People's Campaign co-chair Reverend William Barber held a virtual press conference. Barber said that he and other faith leaders and activists were "willing to engage in a humanitarian visit" to Russia to visit Griner "if the Russian Embassy and the U.S. government would work out the particulars to allow that to happen." Barber then used the term that had been bandied about by many about Griner since her arrest on drug charges in February 2022. He called her a "political pawn."

Barber's proposal almost certainly would suffer the same fate as that of so many others put forth for Griner's release. It would be ignored. Barber predictably got no response from the Russian government. Meanwhile, Griner remained behind bars. That, despite her plea bargain plea of guilty. Her plea bargain at the very least might have made her eligible for a prisoner swap and release which was much talked about.

The problem from the moment Griner was stopped and her bags searched by customs officials in Moscow in February 2022 were that she was not just any alleged criminal offender. She was Black, lesbian, by the standards of women's professional sports in America a genuine celebrity, and a recognized top-tier athlete. She was in Russia again playing for a Russian team to make some semblance of the money. The money that due to the colossal pay inequities between men's and women's pro basketball players, she couldn't make in the U.S.

Her detention came at the moment the U.S. and Russia were engaged in a furious round of charges and countercharges over Russia's brutal war of conquest in Ukraine. The conflict reminded many of the decades-long Cold War conflict between the U.S. and Russia that for more than a half-century at times imperiled the world.

There was no tangible evidence that Griner was being used. as Barber and others charged. as a political pawn or political bait to take the heat off Russia for Ukraine. Or, that she was a bargaining chip. Her celebrity status, though, marked her case as special. If that hadn't been the case, Biden and Vice President Harris, and other top U.S. officials would not have rushed to the barricades and issued statement after statement calling for her release.

Griner would not serve the ten-year sentence legally prescribed for her offense. She would be released. Her celebrity status and the massive support she received within and without the U.S. guaranteed that. Still, Griner stood as yet another example of what happens when the always thorny issues of race, gender, same-sex relations, politics, and in this case war, crash, and clash around one person and one case.

Notes

Introduction

https://www.usatoday.com/story/sports/wnba/mercury/2022/07/18/lebron-james-brittney-griner-comments/10088993002/

https://www.nbcnews.com/politics/biden-preparing-response-brittney-griners-letter-pleading-help-rcna36883

https://www.nbcnews.com/news/vladimir-putin/-terrified-brittney-griner-sends-biden-handwritten-letter-trial-russia-rcna36611

https://blavity.com/gender-pay-gap-sports-brittney-griner

https://fanbuzz.com/nba/wnba-stars-get-better-pay-overseas/

https://www.wsn.com/nba/nba-vs-wnba/

https://venussports.co/2019/07/12/tv-ratings-wnba-fan-attendance-still-lacking/

https://www.huffpost.com/entry/the-wnbas-biggest-problem_b_9437480

2

https://www.nbcnews.com/nbc-out/out-news/russia-makes-failed-attempt-shut-prominent-lgbtq-rights-group-rcna15913

https://www.npr.org/2019/01/14/685192372/activists-say-40-detained-and-2-dead-in-gay-purge-in-chechnya

https://www.msnbc.com/the-reidout/reidout-blog/brittney-griners-identity-makes-prime-target-russia-rcna18981

https://www.cnn.com/2022/03/30/politics/arizona-transgender-health-care-ban-sports-ban/index.html

https://www.essentiallysports.com/nba-basketball-news-brittney-griner-who-has-openly-bashed-gender-norms-once-confessed-ugly-dispute-with-father-accept-your-daughter-and-take-her-for-what-she-is

https://www.cnn.com/2022/03/31/us/brittney-griner-race-deconstructed-newsletter/index.html

https://www.nbcnews.com/feature/nbc-out/brittney-griner-donates-5-000-lgbtq-youth-center-set-fire-n788476

https://www.theguardian.com/sport/2022/jul/14/brittney-griner-trial-wnba-lgbtq-trailblazer

https://thehill.com/changing-america/respect/diversity-inclusion/521709-wnba-star-says-womens-basketball-isnt-popular/

3

https://sports.yahoo.com/former-pentagon-official-russia-could-use-brittney-griner-as-high-profile-hostage-010121886.html

https://www.nbcnews.com/news/us-news/putin-spokesman-says-griner-isnt-hostage-gives-no-hint-release-rcna34462

https://www.aol.com/sports/brittney-griner-political-hostage-russia-210253272.html

https://search.aol.com/aol/search;_ylt=Awr4xJN3_tViDdkAx3tpCWVH;_ylu=Y29sbwNncTEEcG9zAz EEdnRpZAMEc2VjA3BhZ2luYXRpb24-?q=is+griner+a+political+pawn&v_t=loki-keyword&b=11&pz=10&bct=0&xargs=0

https://www.peoplesworld.org/article/u-s-communists-demand-release-of-brittney-griner-end-to-ukraine-war/

https://www.yahoo.com/lifestyle/brittney-griner-russian-trial-adjourned-171938033.html?fr=sycsrp_catchal

Conclusion

https://www.commondreams.org/news/2022/07/15/calling-russia-free-brittney-griner-bishop-barber-seeks-humanitarian-visit

About the Author

Earl Ofari Hutchinson is the author of multiple books on race and politics in America. He is a political analyst. He has appeared on MSNBC and on CNN. His books include the trilogy on the Obama Years: *The Obama Legacy, How Obama Governed; The Year of Crisis and Challenge, and How Obama Won*. His most recent books are *the Trump Challenge to Black America, From King to Obama: Witness to a Turbulent History*. He is the publisher of thehutchinsonreport.net, a political issues web blog.

www.ingramcontent.com/pod-product-compliance
Lightning Source LLC
Chambersburg PA
CBHW070611160726
48003CB00005B/2219